TIPS AND WISDOM ON BEING CAREER SAVVY

Author: Aria Craig

The Single Mother Diaries™
Tips and Wisdom on Being Career Savvy

Volume 2

Copyright © MMXVII by Aria Craig

All rights reserved. No part of this publication may be reproduced, distributed, or transmitted in any form or by any means, including photocopying, recording, or other electronic or mechanical methods, without the prior written permission of the publisher, except in the case of brief quotations embodied in critical reviews and certain other noncommercial uses permitted by copyright law.

MNT Publishing Company, L.L.C.
Crete, IL 60417-0224
www.AriaCraig.com

Design by Image Design Foundry

Printed in the United States of America

ISBN: 978-0-692-93593-4

Copyrighted Material

Prologue

I give all glory and honor to GOD, my Father. Without Him, none of this would be possible. I constantly pray for discernment, patience, understanding and wisdom. I pray for GOD to order my steps in my life when making decisions – especially when those decisions involve others. The Lord dwells in my life and He gets the honor, glory and praise while I accept the victory since my faith is anchored in The Lord - The Author and Finisher of my faith. Proverbs 22: 6 states to train a child in the way he should go and when he is old he will not depart from it.

This volume is dedicated to my grandfather, Samuel Brown. He served this country proudly and was the measure of a man - the one I affectionately called "Daddy". I loved him so much that I named my son after him. I miss him dearly every day and know he is proud of the woman and mother that I have evolved into.

The Single Mother Diaries: Tips and Wisdom on Being Career Savvy

Volume 2

Prologue v

Introduction ix

You and Corporate America

Chapter 1: Climbing the Corporate Ladder of
   Leadership 3
Chapter 2: Key Principles of Working Effectively
   as a Team 11
Chapter 3: The Game – Learn How to Play It 14
Chapter 4: Sharks and Barracudas 16
Chapter 5: Thick-Skinned Bureaucracy 18
Chapter 6: Human Resources (Networking is Key) 22
Chapter 7: Perception vs Reality 24
Chapter 8: Asset vs Liability 26
Chapter 9: Manager vs Leader 29

You and Entrepreneurship

Chapter 10: Corporate America or Entrepreneurship 35
Chapter 11: Find a Coach/Be a Mentor 39
Chapter 12: Key Financial Strategies 43
Chapter 13: Becoming Fearless 47
Chapter 14: Leaving a Legacy 49

You and Being Business Savvy

Chapter 15: Is Leadership Your Calling? 53
Chapter 16: Success is Relative 55
Chapter 17: Manifesting Your Purpose 56
Chapter 18: Conclusion 58

Get in Touch with Aria Craig 59

On The Horizon 61

Introduction

For all the mothers who work tirelessly to create a better living for their children, this book is for you. I worked diligently on this volume to help you define what success means to you in the process of being a fabulous mom!

Do you dream of climbing the corporate ladder, but convinced yourself that you are not ready or worthy because of all your priorities as a mom? Within these pages you'll learn about leadership, how the different levels in a company achieve results, and what you can do to move into that next leadership role as an aspiring mom. You'll also learn about how to avoid sharks and barracudas along the way and understand the difference between being a manager and a leader.

This book is also for you moms who dream about starting your own business, but convinced yourself that it's too late, too difficult, or you don't have enough funds. And what about those who have been betrayed by Corporate America? Who sacrificed time with their children, getting to work extra early and staying extra late to make an impression, or dealing with unnerving office politics - this book is for you! Transfer those skills into your own business, build your own clientele, and hire your own staff. Value and validate yourself!

I share my personal experiences in the corporate world and how I overcame incredibly challenging obstacles before discovering the entrepreneur journey I was destined to embark. This book is meant to stir your desires and motivate your heart to the point to where you become very intentional about making that leap.

Now, let's get started!

YOU AND CORPORATE AMERICA

Chapter One

Climbing the Corporate Ladder of Leadership

Many people dream of having that huge office with the cherry oak desk, windows overlooking the lake or downtown, and a secretary that handles the flow of calls and visitors. But, is this really the route that you want to take? Yes, you are a parent that may be single, divorced or part of a blended-family household who already has a lot of responsibilities. But, if you are determined to reach your goals of promotion and success in the corporate environment, then being laser-focused when you walk through the doors of the building is extremely important. The willingness to do it all while balancing home life takes a lot of strength and commitment. Getting to that next level involves being confident, assertive, and ready to transform your mindset as a leader.

Having these attributes may stretch you past your comfort zone. To go above and beyond the status quo. Tackle fear head on and consume it. Think about it. Just as you find different ways to encourage your children's growth, you must do the same for yourself. You coach them to build confidence and reach for greater heights. The same goes for you. Create a list of professional goals, then use the following tips to help you transition into your next leadership role. Along the way, you'll find that these tips will be assets in the workplace as well as in your home, where you also operate in the role of a leader.

If you are currently a staff employee or lead others:

1. Start surrounding yourself with people who not only aspire to do greater things with their lives, but are actually *working* towards it. Their energy and drive should manifest itself in such a way that it becomes contagious and encourages you to formulate ideas towards your own definition of success. Your ambition can be seen in taking the lead in new and challenging responsibilities in your department, or in learning more about how the department, and company, operates.

2. Create short and long-term goals. The professionals that I coach complete this task and designate accountability partners with whom they have regular conversations about whether or not they are moving towards the right direction in achieving results.

3. Get insight from your immediate supervisor about your strengths and how you can improve. Even your peers can offer a perspective that you hadn't

seen before. Use their feedback as an opportunity to reassess your career plan and make adjustments.

4. Develop a mental model that you are going to have a positive attitude throughout your day. There will always be moments of stress, irritation and mediocrity in the workplace. The key is how well you handle these situations. Your leaders are paying attention to your response because it determines your level of professionalism of this important soft skill.

5. Operate with creative thinking. Show your supervisor or management staff that you understand how processes work and that you have ideas on how to streamline them, cut costs, save the company money, increase revenue, etc. Anything that displays your ability to think outside the box and problem solve demonstrates leadership abilities.

6. Be proactive in providing support in your department. Not only does this display teamwork, but also a willingness to take the lead so the entire department can succeed.

7. Find a mentor in the industry you are pursuing. A mentor understands your career track and will offer advice on how to reach your goals. Most people select someone at least three positions

above them. It is significant when someone who has an incredibly busy schedule is willing to take time to advocate for you and help you develop. However, it is not a bad idea to find someone who is at the next level of leadership, because the higher up the corporate ladder, the focus shifts from actually delivering results to "how" those results are delivered. Someone in a position three or more levels higher than you may not remember the ins and outs of what your next position of leadership requires. For instance, a vice president of a division may not recall the details of the assistant manager position they held five years ago. The communication, interaction with line staff, and decision-making are all different at that level. Lower level management is concerned with the direction of their department and the performance of their team to meet the goals cascaded to them from higher levels. Executives, on the other hand, are making decisions regarding the direction of the organization, aligning its vision, and supporting the demands of sponsors and stakeholders. Their focus is on branding, strategy and net worth. It doesn't hurt to have mentors that are both one and three (plus) levels ahead of you.

If you are currently a manager:

1. Develop a level of trust, respect and accountability amongst your peers and immediate supervisor. Your team needs to feel that you value their performance and recognize their hard work, listen to their ideas and pain points, encourage empowerment and innovation, offer constructive feedback, and admit when you have made mistakes. Most managers that I've worked for passed the blame to their employees, which created dissatisfaction, discord, and distrust. Just about everyone in the department regularly used company time to look for another job opportunity. Your goal should be team cohesiveness.

2. Create strategies to develop your employees and invest in their career growth. Staff that want to eventually advance to a leadership role will need your support in moving forward, not holding back.

3. Value your team by recognizing their talents and advocating for them. Because it is your responsibility to ensure the success of your team, knowing each employee's strength shows the executive team that you are an expert in delegation and understand the vision. In addition, it'll prepare you to designate the best lead for your department, thus providing valuable support. This is part of the decision-making skills needed in leaders.

4. Develop conflict resolution strategies. This is important because not all conflict is bad. You should encourage an environment in which constructive criticism is respectful and leads to achieving team goals. It can actually motivate employees, if handled successfully. The way you handle this can be a huge factor in determining your ability to move to the next level in leadership.

5. Communicate effectively. This is a tremendous strength of winning managers. Whether it is giving feedback for a performance review or conveying a message from the top down regarding organizational change, you are the middle person and it is your responsibility to bridge the gap between executive level and the staff level. Communication is essential to any relationship and is only successful when your message is relayed in a manner that's clearly understood and you are listening intently to responses from your team to understand their view.

If you are currently an executive:

Create a clear and concise vision for your organization so that all key players know their target. Whether you are the director of a division or the president of an entire organization, you cannot effectively lead anyone without successfully communicating a direction. It is your responsibility to ensure that everyone who reports to you effectively communicates this vision to their departments and develops strategies on how to reach that destination.

1. Be a mentor for aspiring visionaries, CEO's, and executive directors. These professionals are the cream of the crop and are depending on your wisdom and expertise to learn how to manage the pressures at your level; build, sustain and leverage relationships with other executives; use authority to influence instead of abuse; balance a highly-visible position with home life obligations; and bounce back from failures then use them as stepping stones for success.

2. Acknowledge the contributions of your employees. It is because of them that the department is functioning, so recognizing their efforts makes them eager to your leadership.

3. Adopt a confident and charismatic personality. Some of the most successful leaders in the world are ones that are fascinating and inspiring with a high level of assurance. It is easier for people to resonate with and become drawn to them, thus have a desire to follow them.

4. Effectively communicate change. Honesty with diplomacy is essential. After all, with so much uncertainty over job loss employees are checking media platforms often to find the future state of

their organization. There should be effective communication cascaded down through leadership.

5. Be committed and resilient. Employees need to see that their leader will not only advocate for them and direct them to greater heights, but stand with the organization in times of setbacks and quickly recover from adversity.

6. Ensure honesty and integrity. These may arguably be the most important attributes of a strong leader. Being ethical and unwavering on your stand for what is right creates an atmosphere that yields loyalty and pride for employees of any organization.

All these qualities of effective leaders in Corporate America can be leveraged in the household as well. You'll want to model these values for your children to guide their influence of leadership.

Chapter Two

Key Principles of Working Effectively as a Team

The summer after my son graduated from eighth grade, he and I had a conversation about expectations in high school - what I expected from him, what his teachers would expect from him, and what he could expect in the next four years. Other than taking on more challenging coursework, there was one thing that stood out more than others. He noticed how often his teachers placed their students in teams to complete class and homework assignments (an expectation I mentioned to him). He then understood that he was learning several leadership skills that would help prepare him for the workforce:

1. How well he worked with others. Just like his teachers, managers need to see how well he is able to work with people whose behaviors are different than his. Effectively managing various personalities is about 80% of a leader's role.

2. How to view creativity from someone else's perspective. His views are different from those on his team. Seeing things from another person's perspective yields more ideas and bolder outcomes while creating synergy.

3. How to determine each team member's strengths to delegate tasks effectively. If my son is more artistic, another team member loves to research, and the third member has a passion for public speaking, then it would be more effective for the second team member to research key points, my son to create the PowerPoint slides, while his third team mate spoke through the presentation. That way it is a win/win for the entire team.

4. When to pull more than his own weight. There will always be times when he feels as though he put forth more of an effort than someone on his team. Like his teacher, his manager will expect him to figure out how to resolve this issue because the bottom line is achieving the goal.

5. How to work together to complete an assignment. Getting together to create a plan of action is critical. Each person will know their part of the assignment and be held accountable for executing the strategy, which includes juggling different priorities.

6. How to motivate each other to meet deadlines. Encouraging each other helps the team to perform at its best.

7. How to resolve issues and address critical ones with his teachers. They are expecting him to resolve issues on his own. After all, problem-solving is a critical skill of every leader. Just as in school, only when he has exercised all options and cannot come to an agreement to meet goals is when issues should be addressed with his manager in a timely fashion.

Any company that has more than one person doing all the work operates as a team. As a leader, these are key principles when working together as a team to meet a common goal. Executing them efficiently and effectively will help you demonstrate how prepared you are to move to the next level in your organization.

Chapter Three

The Game – Learn How to Play It

If you have the drive to move up the corporate ladder, then understand that the attributes from Chapter 1 are the apparent rules. But, there are also some unmentioned ones that make this a game where only the strongest survive.

What I have realized while working in Corporate America is that, all too often, office politics are the pathway to higher positions, even if the expertise does not warrant it. I was told, as mentioned earlier, that leadership roles are 80% personality and 20% expertise – not only having the ability to work well with others, but more importantly, the ability to build relationships with other leaders. Of course, if you're awarded a position based on your talents and skills, that's great! However, if that promotion is offered to a person who is obviously less qualified, but has a personal relationship with the hiring manager, then that's a different story.

In my last place of employment, I witnessed too many people in the department gaining a competitive edge because they fraternized with the boss, bought her gifts and even traveled out of town with her on personal trips. I wasn't considered for promotion because I didn't play their game. It was demoralizing and played on my self-esteem. It made me feel valueless. It was if they were trying to box me in, a person full of ambition. I lost respect for the department and the organization. The situation eventually affected my health, which manifested itself in how I managed my family affairs.

If you experience scenarios like this for an extended period of time, it might be best to transition to a different department or to another company altogether. Don't waste your time giving so much of your excellence to a department that does not value your strengths and talents. You are worth more and can only sharpen yourself with others who are willing to invest in what you have to offer.

Chapter Four

Sharks and Barracudas

A shark's method of attack is to sneak up from below and strike upwards in a vertical motion at its unsuspecting prey. They are considered apex predators, which means they are at the top of the food chain. A barracuda's method is to slowly hunt at the bottom, mostly at night, then shoot out to attack its prey. They are considered scavengers and cannibals, and are attracted to shiny objects.

Corporate America is full of sharks and barracudas. Employees who possess shark-like character traits are usually in high positions in the organization. They smile in your face and welcome you into their offices to converse about personal issues. But, they will use any opportunity while your guard is down to strike in an effort to harm your position in the company. They abuse their power as authority figures in the waters of the organization. They move up the corporate ladder by any means necessary, even if that means launching attacks to lessen anybody else's chances at the same opportunity of survival within the organization.

Barracudas in Corporate America are those peers that listen to your feedback in meetings, then relay that same feedback to higher-ups as if they created the ideas themselves. They sit with you at lunch, coffee breaks, work functions, and even personal events, listening to you talk about your frustrations with management and your career goals. Then they go directly to your manager to reveal what you shared in confidence so they get that same promotion (the "shiny object") that you worked so hard to achieve. Those types of employees will harm you and any other peer in order to get to the top.

Let's just face it. As a working woman, you will encounter all types of people in the workforce. Some will mean well and some will try to do harm. Trust me. If you are a career-minded mother, using caution when working with these types of individuals is key to your happiness, peace of mind, and success. This type of predatory behavior extends to personal encounters. But, you can choose to be different. Dare to be different and have integrity. Don't allow sharks and barracudas to influence your decision making at work or home. Instead turn your workplace ordeal into something positive and teach your child the importance of working for accomplishments, but not at the cost of others.

Chapter Five

Thick-Skinned Bureaucracy

Single mothers working in Corporate America face a unique set of tough challenges. We deal with tons of stresses factors in our personal lives and have to work incredibly hard to not comingle them with the workplace. Because of this there are co-workers who are less than empathetic to our situations and try to sabotage any chance of progression.

Corporate America has its share of bullies, which is why having thick skin is crucial to your survival. I once worked at a healthcare conglomerate that had excellent perks and benefits, but the department was the worst in all my years of employment. The managers made emotional decisions and promoted people based on friendship. If you were not part of their circle, then you were not getting promoted. Individuals who were not even half as qualified were pulled up the corporate ranks simply because they were friends with a senior manager or executive. Meanwhile, other employees were immediately put on "the list" if they exhibited any resistance to the department whose culture was based on the three F's: fear, favoritism and fraternizing (which, by the way, was against company policy).

This became a hostile work environment. Several employees gained the reputation of being poisonous because they spread rumors and influenced other team members to become rebellious by performing at substandard levels and refusing to take on any new challenges. Then there were managers who smiled in the faces of their staff members, promoted an open-door policy where employees could discuss concerns and personal issues, then gossiped with other managers about the private information that was told to them in confidence (sharks). The sad part is that these people still hold positions in that department and most of them continue to climb up the corporate ladder, not caring about the amount of distress they've caused under their leadership.

I eventually lost respect for those managers. For years, I worked all kinds of hours, sacrificing time with my son in order to build the reputation of being dependable, hard-working, efficient, and a valuable team player. In the end, the accolades, monetary rewards, and promotions were awarded to other employees – including one who had grammatical and spelling challenges, barracuda-like characteristics, and struggled with personal hygiene (so much that grievances were filed by other co-workers) – just because she worshipped our manager.

I had to exercise my rights as an employee and contact Human Resources. From that point forward, my manager saw me as a threat. She refused to recognize my talents, would not promote me (which was also against company policy), and placed me in a cubicle in front of the same office that she gave the employee with poor hygiene.

How could this happen? I had worked just as hard as she did and ran a single-family home in the process. The hardest part was the realization that the time I didn't spend with my child while trying to prove myself to this department was time I would never get back: a clear lesson that life wasn't fair. There were times I wanted to cry, but I had to remain strong in the presence of my son. Every day I would have to adjust my demeanor so that he was not exposed to my anger and frustration. He didn't see me as an employee enduring trials and tribulations at this company that was also helping me provide food, shelter and clothing - his needs and wants. He saw me as Mommy. His hero. His protector. His security blanket.

After hearing some of the same horror stories from other people at this company, I realized that I had to redirect my focus. I would see others in the lobby walking around without a sign of distress, as if they loved their jobs. I needed to get there fast because the stress was taking a toll on me physically, psychologically and emotionally. It even made me question my level of faith. I knew that I needed to develop thicker skin. I couldn't ignore that these issues were occurring, but I had to redirect them to positive energy so that I could allow myself to experience my God-given right to joy. To walk around with a smile on my face and not allow myself to feel defeated.

I'm glad to say that I no longer see my value through the eyes of others. I define myself through my own actions. The renewed faith I developed from my bad experiences led me to start doing what I love to do and focus on the manifestation process. Now, my son gets happy when he sees me working on what brings me the most joy, which is helping other mothers use their setbacks as stepping stones towards being in alignment with their purpose. The most important lesson I learned from all of this is how to value and validate myself.

Chapter Six

Human Resources (Networking is Key)

Anyone at a supervisory level or higher will tell you that networking is a key part of gaining promotion momentum in the corporate world. Grabbing a cup of coffee, taking a lunch break, or attending an after-work event with someone from a different department are great ways to build connections with folks outside of your own work setting. And it doesn't necessarily have to be someone at a higher level than you. Creating a great impression and solidifying that network can yield great friendships and links to other opportunities that may present themselves in the future.

Every person I have witnessed moving up the corporate ladder had some type of relationship that extended past, "Here are the results of that report you requested." Now, that doesn't mean you should rush to invite your boss over for dinner or even go as far as to compromise your integrity to get to that next level. It means take time to get to know your manager a little more. For starters, what are her hobbies or where has she traveled? Share positive experiences about parenthood. These are chances to build relationships and bridge gaps.

If you are uncomfortable with having that type of relationship with your manager, then I completely understand. Some people are hesitant because they fear that what their manager knows about them personally could possibly be used against them personally. That's a legitimate concern. I know firsthand of situations in which people spilled their personal pains out to their managers, only to have that information used against them during performance reviews when deciding if they would be able to handle more responsibility. But, your manager doesn't have to be the only point of connection. If you work in a mid-size or large company, then go forth and build strong connections with other managers or executives. That may be your next leadership breakthrough!

Chapter Seven

Perception vs Reality

"Don't let someone else's perception become your reality." These were the words of wisdom given to me from a former manager. In other words, you cannot allow another person's opinion of you to define you. Unless there is some truth and you see those patterns within yourself, you should take someone else's view lightly.

Be the creator of your own destiny. Only you can determine the direction in which you decide to go in life. If you make changes within yourself, then keep the best interest of you (and your child) in mind - no one else should influence your decision. Change should be something that you embrace when you realize there is a need for improvement, not for validation.

If you really want to find out what areas need developing professionally, there are plenty of assessment tools that identify your strengths and areas for improvement. One tool that is effective in large companies is the 360°Profile™. It has a dynamic function that crosses multiple levels. It is completed by your supervisor, peers, and those that report to you to help you understand your strengths and identify where there is room for change. Each level will have a different perspective of your leadership skills because you relate to them differently.

Chapter Eight

Asset vs Liability

An asset is defined as something or someone that is useful or can provide value. When we think of assets, we think of them in a positive sense. After all, you are an asset every day at home, you own assets, and you surround yourself with people who would be of asset to you. The same goes for companies. They are always searching for candidates who will add value to their goals and vision.

As an employee, you can use those qualities you have mastered in your experience as a mom to triumph in your role. Multi-tasking, leading, and making important decisions are all skills that you already possess. Why not use them as an all-encompassing tool for the workplace? Ask questions. Volunteer to assist your teammate. Be proactive. Establish positive relationships with other employees in the company – including those not in your department. Show a willingness to learn. These are all characteristics that employers view when determining the resources they will need, those they will let go, and who has the potential to move up the organization.

A liability, on the other hand, is quite different. It is defined as the state of being held legally responsible for someone or something. We typically do not favor liabilities because they pose too much of a risk or incur too much debt. You deal with liabilities every day. You may serve as a liability when posting negative comments about the company you work for on social media, constantly making personal phone calls, yielding a low performance, being rude, and gossiping. Your employer may begin to rethink the level of value that you add to the department and view you as a risk.

Some employers perceive a liability when they see mothers who constantly take off to deal with emergencies involving their child (by the way, FMLA may be an option to help you keep your job while taking off to tend to your sick child.) These are circumstances that you will want to keep to a minimum. Have back-up plans, such as your child's father, a close relative, or friend that is reliable in the event that you need their support.

I once worked for a company that required employees to work nearly every Saturday during the last quarter of the year to accommodate year-end close activities. For the first four years I was allowed to bring my son into the office while I worked. I made sure I equipped him with crayons, coloring books, a CD player, and any other useful activities that would keep him occupied while I focused on my tasks. The fact that I brought him in on those mandatory weekends made my manager cognizant of my hard work, sacrifice, and leaderships kills. It gave the perception that I was a diligent and committed employee who took pride in my performance (which in turn, made her look good as a manager).

But, because my manager did not have children she was less accepting when I was unable to be in the office due to health issues with my son. I made sure to communicate everything to her so that there weren't any surprises. Yet, all of a sudden I was told during my last year of employment that I was no longer able to bring my son with me on Saturdays because the company thought he would be a liability. He stayed with his dad every other weekend, but I still had to find someone willing to watch him for a full Saturday on the weekends that he was with me. I did not have much success, so I had no choice but to find a job that was not as demanding. Needless to say, I went from being an asset to the company to a liability (and apparently, so did my son).

So ask yourself these questions, "What value can I add to the company? What part can I play in making sure that the department meets its goals? Or does my department see me as being radioactive and toxic?" If you and your manager see the value that you add, then congratulations! If your actions do not translate, then you have some work to do!

Chapter Nine

Manager vs Leader

I have worked for a few awesome managers in my years, but the longer I work in Corporate America, the more I am convinced that some leaders are clueless about the difference between being a manager and being a leader. Managers define objectives, delegate tasks, monitor production, measure progress, and disciple employees. Their objective is to get the work done and measure results. A leader, however, understands that they are a stimulus. They do everything a manager does, but their objective is to coach, empower, and motivate in order to cultivate a more enriched and engaged team. Managers use power to control. Leaders use power to influence.

If you are in a position of authority, then do yourself a favor and build your leadership skills. It's not just your team that's monitoring your moves and seeing how well you perform under pressure. Other people in the organization are watching you, too. Take a close look at other leaders in your organization and even those in the public eye. What characteristics do they possess? Are there certain styles that you can emulate in your growth and development?

Employees are most diligent about effectively carrying out their roles when they know they are being heard, valued, and respected. When they can share their ideas without being criticized or constantly rejected. When their hard work is seen and rewarded. When the feedback they receive is for their growth. When their managers advocate for them, challenge them, and value them enough to invest in their development, promotion, and success.

It is your job as part of leadership to create a culture that keeps employees satisfied without breaking company policy. Employees who are happy at their jobs can agree that these factors contribute to their decision to stay with their employer:

- Competitive pay, benefits, and incentives
- Potential to transfer into a career
- Work culture that fosters trust, integrity and creativity
- Room for growth / advancement
- Diversity and inclusion

- Leadership behavior consistent with culture and values

- Mentorship and development programs

- Work/life balance

- Timely and constructive feedback (that motivates)

- Recognition / awards for excellent performance

- Flexibility with schedule

- Autonomy in working independently

Think about it. As a manager or leader, could you respond well to someone you report to who constantly shuts you down, takes credit for your work, or shows favor to other employees who aren't as knowledgeable about the department as you are? At some point, wouldn't you eventually become disgruntled enough to search for another job? Lead your team in a manner that reduces office politics and demonstrates two-way need. They want your guidance and support; you need their efforts and experience. Having both needs met leads to the creation of the three S's: satisfaction, synergy, and success.

YOU AND ENTREPRENEURSHIP

Chapter Ten

Corporate America or Entrepreneurship

After working at that well-known insurance company for five years and realizing that I was being black-balled, I had to figure out another plan. So, I started looking for another job. My thoughts were to apply for positions one or two grade levels higher than my current position. After all, I felt I was qualified, but was being treated unfairly.

Initially, I applied for positions within the company. Next, I applied outside the company (while still searching internally). Each time I applied and was not considered, a piece of me was broken. My emotional and psychological health was being compromised. I began to devalue myself and became bitter towards those who blocked my growth. At one point, one of my managers actually told me that she would not recommend me for another position. This created work-related stress for another three years.

Around that second year, I had an epiphany. I figured it was as good a time as any to start writing my books. I jotted down notes, opened my laptop and started cranking out paragraphs. Paragraphs became chapters. Chapters became a book. I was now a writer. I opened up a business account and started investing in ways to self-publish.

Around that third year, I was diagnosed with anxiety and depression. I took a short-term leave to seek treatment. One month turned into two. Then two months turned into three. Before I knew it, I was out for six months! The doctors and therapists were insistent on prescribing me anti-anxiety pills and anti-depressants to help me "handle" returning back to work, but I was reluctant to take the latter. During this time, I continued to work on my book series, The Single Mother Diaries™. Because I had always wanted to be an author, I was not surprised to find this process to be therapeutic and fulfilling.

Eventually, I returned to work because I felt the need to prove my worth and value once more. To not accept defeat. After all, that is exactly what my manager and her manager wanted. However, after being back for only a couple of months, my symptoms flared up again. My body went into fight or flight mode and my health got worse than the first time around. I couldn't understand why the company (ironically, in the health insurance industry) did not investigate and take action to correct the obvious problems in the department that led to me (and others) having to take leave for the same illness. I was forced to go back on leave for a second time and lost my job. It took a while for me to understand that my integrity and values could not withstand a culture based on fear, intimidation, and disrespect of its own policies.

Being on leave due to work-related stress actually influenced me to refocus on my purpose. It was time to be intentional! After publishing my book and selling the very first one (to my husband), I was officially an author! It wasn't until then that I realized I was also an entrepreneur.

Understand that being an entrepreneur is not for everyone. Some people are comfortable with a company being already established to secure their salaries with benefits. Owning your own business is even more challenging because not only are you (or your partner) filling every role and investing way more time into getting it established, but the success of your company depends entirely on you. However, if owning your own business makes you warm and tingly inside then go for it! And if you have a job or career, then by all means do not leave it unless you deem it necessary. Use that as an opportunity to finance your own business. If you don't have that luxury, then find ways to finance your business (family and friends, crowdfunding, microlenders, investors, venture capitalists, and sponsorship from major corporations, etc.). I was clear on my direction, so I borrowed money from my 401(k) (please consult an advisor before going this route).

You would be surprised how aggressive you will become to earn revenue when you start from an angle of being broke!

Your experience may not be as dramatic as mine. My circumstances forced me to assess some things in my life and transform my thinking for my own sake and the sake of my family. If it had not happened, I would still be giving my all to a company that was undeserving of my talents. Bound to a company that was not bound to me. Even worse, my health would have declined even more. My journey to become an entrepreneur was not evident, at first. But, I quickly learned that those Corporate America skills I honed were transferable. I now use them to grow my own business instead of someone else's.

Chapter Eleven

Find a Coach/Be a Mentor

If establishing your own company has been a dream, then right now is the time to activate it. Being a busy working mom and taking care of your children should not deter you, but motivate you. Use it as an incentive to create a legacy and new sense of pride. But, first you need someone that will help direct you up the right path towards success and hold you accountable. A business coach, specifically one with that industry's expertise, would be a valuable investment. As a business coach myself, I invite you to explore three high-level steps to help you manage your decision.

Step 1: Get Clarity

Clarity is one of the first steps to establishing your own business. Believe it or not, most people know they want to work for themselves, but have no clue what they want to do. Some people have an epiphany after realizing that a large demographic has a specific need or problem that's still not quite solved and they have the solution.

The defining moment of truth is when you assess what excites you and combine it with your talents to get in alignment. Get in a quiet space to meditate or reflect on things in your life that jolt you and make you dream in the first place. Once you've gained clarity, then you're ready to move to the next step.

Step 2: Transform Your Dreams to Goals

Now that you know which direction you want to travel, it's time to start the transformation process. Some people struggle with a straightforward conversion from dreams to goals. Therefore, I've added another stage. Convert those dreams into ideas first. Begin physically writing out the ideas that you have for your business. For instance, travel, speak, blog, community service, etc." Next, convert those ideas into goals and write them out in complete sentences. For example, "My designing business will allow me to travel across the world," or "My non-profit organization will service low-income communities across the Midwest".

Next, dig deeper and specify the core products or services that you will provide in your company. No need to have everything right away. You can always build as you go. Lastly, put your vision on a dream board or list somewhere in plain view (your bathroom mirror, your bedroom walls, your laptop screen), so that you see it every day. Your vision will depict what you want to accomplish with your business.

Step 3: Develop an Action Plan

This is the step where the bulk of your time will be spent in developing your business. It is the blueprint for how you will get it up and running, gain clientele/customers, and retain them. It has a lot of moving pieces because you are constantly revising it to see what works and what doesn't.

Carve out time to write out a business plan, which will help you identify your target market, market analysis, branding strategies, competitor analysis and risks, budget and future financial projections (like Income Statement, Cash Flow Statement, Balance Sheet, and Return on Investment). Don't feel overwhelmed. It seems like a lot, but it is essential because it helps determine how you plan to manage your business and how well it is performing financially. Most people create these to get financing for their companies. If you are going to bootstrap your company, then you won't need to create all the components, but they will be extremely helpful to monitor progress. Again, it serves as a blueprint so you are not taking steps blindly. If you need help with a template The Small Business Administration has a very comprehensive business plan template. A business coach should be able to walk you through each step.

Do not forget to develop a home/work life balance plan. Create a schedule for you and your children, then stick to it. If your son has a football game at 3 p.m. on a weeknight and your daughter has an 11 a.m. recital on Saturday, then you will need to block out time that week to focus on business tasks and time to join them for their events/activities. Also make sure to take time out just to pamper yourself. Get a massage and facial, plan a weekend getaway (with your spouse, kids or just friends), go see a play, participate in a wine and paint party or simply soak in a bubble bath while listening to relaxing music. You need to allow yourself time to decompress and renew your mind so that you are rejuvenated (also noted in Volume One of The Single Mother Diaries™).

Chapter Twelve

Key Financial Strategies

Included within your business plan are key financial strategies. They are the financial actuals and projections of your blueprint. You should not only set financial goals, but budget for them. Have a clear amount that you want to spend for each operational piece. As the saying goes, "it takes money to make money." Planning your moves helps you make the best investment decisions for your company. Your business coach should be able to assist you with this process. But, be patient. Rome wasn't built in a day and neither will your business be.

At the beginning, you will want to establish what type of business you will become (LLC, partnership, sole proprietorship, etc.). Depending on which state you live in, this decision can be expensive.

In addition, you want to create your business name and open a business account. Come up with a very creative slogan and logo, then get them trademarked. If you can operate your business from home, that will alleviate a ton of overhead expenses. If not, then budget for space. When acquiring space, ask if it includes awnings or a marquee where you can display your business name. Budget for equipment and manufacturing prototypes, if your business is product-driven. Put an ad in the local papers to let them know that you are open for business.

Branding is a fundamental piece that a lot of entrepreneurs slack on in their budget. I've noticed over time that the bulk of my expenses were allocated toward my marketing efforts to build my brand. Thus, it should be part of your marketing strategy. A business coach can help you identify the best options for creating your brand. Business cards, flyers, contracts, welcome packets and posters can be part of your marketing materials. A lot of companies create inexpensive yet quality marketing products such as these. There's also the need to develop your website or landing page and hosting (which can get expensive). Find a reputable web designer to assist you. Social group memberships are a great way to network and get your name out there. Keep in mind that there is a difference between marketing and branding. Marketing is the process of building the exposure while branding is the process of building the perception.

Now, it's time to do some research. Learn what your competitors are doing that's making them successful. Find out their fees or prices, services, and freebies they provide. Their marketing strategies, color scheme, and content in their marketing that are capturing their audience. Then brainstorm how you can provide your services in such a unique way that you stand out above and beyond your competitors. What product or services can you provide to your potential clients for free (yes, free) so that they can get the opportunity to sample what you have to offer before they commit? As my business coach told me, people will only buy from those they know and trust.

In addition, start creating your fee or price structure for your products or services. Your fees should not be so low that people will not value what you have to offer, nor so high that they cannot afford them. Again, do research and create fees or prices according to the industry market and your experience. In the beginning (and every so often), you may have to give your product or service for free (like a giveaway or a contest, etc.) and follow-up with something they will be willing to pay for. Remember, don't offer too much for free and don't offer it too often. Free does not pay the bills! The purpose is to entice your audience by giving them a taste of what you have to offer to solve their problem. And if you have the opportunity, ask them to offer feedback that you can put on your website, business card, book, etc. This is a great exchange!

Social media is crucial to your marketing strategy. The ad campaigns are not cheap, so the best way is to build your network and connect to it for free. Start creating a buzz to let people know that you are about to launch your product or services. Get them engaged in online dialogue so you can find out their interests. Connect with other groups and possibly comment on other peoples' blogs to create exposure. Utilize all of your free avenues and link them to other platforms (such as your website). Then, start advertising on social media. And remember, social media is a strategy that should be consistent and continuous.

Besides the cost of developing a tangible product and the equipment or services you will use to create it, you have to budget for expenses such as office supplies, postage, software, computer(s), overhead expenses, etc. Include the costs of an attorney, accountant, and insurance.

There are other details to consider (such as focus groups, manufacturers of the product, and possible partnerships), but remember that your business coach is there to help guide you through your start-up journey and beyond. They guide you through creating plans and strategies, then hold you accountable for implementation. They should also be part of the nurturing process afterwards to acknowledge your progress. Learn from your mistakes (there will be plenty), and celebrate your wins.

Chapter Thirteen

Becoming Fearless

Have courage, faith, patience and determination through this journey of entrepreneurship. There will be times when you question your decision and want to give up. There will be times when you fail at a particular process. But, you have to remain fearless! Don't allow trepidation to consume you and don't make emotional decisions. The most noted celebrities suffered failures along the way. Why not learn from them and apply that type of thinking to your process? That's part of the journey towards success.

Confidence in your strengths will take you far. Not only will you develop other strengths, but others will see it and gravitate to you. In the meantime, be careful not to compare yourself to anyone else. Don't impose someone else's current state on your future state. Their journey and the length of time it took them to get there is different from yours. Embrace your own experiences and let that fuel you.

Part of being fearless is being audacious. Hone in on your target market and be intentional about it. This is extremely important because only a certain type of person will fit into your category to buy your products or services. Your slogan to your business should not only be unique enough to stand out over your competitors, but it should cater to your potential client and their needs. Therefore, make sure you invest in understanding their problems. If a person does not believe that you are of value to solve their problems, then they will not invest their time or money into your business.

Chapter Fourteen

Leaving a Legacy

All of these strategies show a great deal of leadership. They demonstrate your determination to not give up and your zeal to make an imprint on future generations. Your children will see your drive. They will appreciate your blood, sweat, and tears. They won't forget how your hard work and sacrifices made certain luxuries available to them. They will see the development of your character and start to emulate those leadership qualities. Pride and honor will resonate in their souls because they will have a parent that overcame obstacles for their sake. Even better is the boost in self-respect and self-confidence that you will develop. You will believe that you can do anything you set your mind to. And that's the exact message you want to show your children.

The SINGLE MOTHER Diaries
Tips and Wisdom on Being Career Savvy
Vol. 2

YOU AND BEING BUSINESS SAVVY

Chapter Fifteen

Is Leadership Your Calling?

Are you the type of person that needs to implement new strategies, not be part of a status quo? Do you have an innate need to serve others? Those are all qualities of leaders. They have a unique charisma and think outside of the box. They have a certain level of influence and understand their impact on others. They share their experiences and guide without hand-holding. They are accountable and foster integrity. They nurture, serve and advocate. They don't like being stagnant and are constantly striving for excellence. They see the bigger picture and are always challenging themselves to do more. Do better. Accomplish greater.

Do those characteristics describe you, or are you someone who sits by the sidelines? Do you wait to be told what to do and how to do it? Do you create an atmosphere of negativity? Are you complacent and only care about what's in it for you? Do you fear challenges and have no established short or long-term success goals? Then being in a leadership role may not be for you. You are doing just enough to get by. Some people don't want to deal with the risk or responsibility that leadership roles require. That is fine, as long as that thinking is not imposed on others who are called to lead. If leading is part of your purpose, you'll know.

Chapter Sixteen

Success is Relative

Everyone has their own definition of success. Fancy cars, huge houses on acres of land, private jets, pricey jewelry - these are objects that wealthy people possess, but that doesn't mean that these things define success. Let's face it, there are a lot people who live in houses and drive cars that they really can't afford, all because they want to give the perception that they have reached a certain level in their lives.

Figure out what you must achieve in order to reach your own definition of success. That might mean taking on your 100th client, branching out your business, or landing a VP opportunity. However, don't measure your level of success by what someone else obtains. Sure, the achievements of others can be motivation for you, but that should be the exception, not the rule. Get motivated by the determination and drive fueled by your own experiences in life. Once you reach a level of success that you pictured for yourself, go out and celebrate!

Chapter Seventeen

Manifesting Your Purpose

We all have either heard of or participated in vision board parties where people come together with boards, paste, tape, and magazines or books to create a collage of what they envision for their future. The key is to not create this board or plan from your current state, but to remove the limitations off your mind and envision your goals on a much larger scale. Turn those visions into goals and start tackling them as if they were absolute (destined as reality).

I have two vision boards - one propped against the mirror on the dresser in my bedroom and the other as my desktop screensaver. The latter was intentional so that I could see it whenever I opened my laptop to do work with the ability to take it with me wherever I traveled. Since I'm more of a fan of writing things out than crafting, I have a dry erase board where I list out my short and long-term goals, immediate tasks, affirmations, and mantra. I keep it in my bedroom next to my dresser so that I see it every single day. I also have an affirmation that my husband wrote for me on a stick-it note I placed on my bathroom mirror and another one on the dashboard of my car. I break down my vision into goals and work on them as if they are already destined to manifest and I am taking the necessary steps to make it happen.

My firm belief is that if we believe in something so strongly, we will put in the work, then see those divine connections and opportunities begin to unfold. It is just as Habakkuk 2:2-3 reads, "Write down the vision and make it plain on tablets so that a herald may run to it. For the vision awaits an appointed time; but in the end it will speak and it will not lie. Though it lingers, wait for it; for it will certainly come and will not delay. " Transforming your dreams into a reality means writing your vision out as a plan, then work diligently on it to manifest.

Chapter Eighteen

Conclusion

The desires you have for yourself and your children are worth more than anything. You only have one life to live, so why not live each day bettering yourself and others in the process? Whether climbing up the corporate ladder is important to you, starting that dream establishment that's been lingering in your soul, or both, one thing is for certain: the leadership development that these journeys bring will catapult you to new levels and into an opportunity to transform your thinking from the mindset you had yesterday.

Want more? Get the ***Being Career Savvy Workbook*** to accompany your reading and begin your journey towards walking in your purpose as a leader.

Get in Touch with Aria Craig

As a speaker and experienced consultant in project management, Aria developed programs to propel the career-driven and entrepreneur mom towards success through group coaching, online programs, and speaking engagements.

*** Remember to pick up your Best-Selling copy of *The Single Mother Diaries™, Volume 1: Tips and Wisdom on Being a Fabulous and Successful Single Mother*

For information on booking Aria Craig for a speaking engagement or hosting a workshop for your group, church, conference, or organization, please contact her by:
Phone: (877) 534-4293
Email: aria@ariacraig.com
Website: www.AriaCraig.com

On The Horizon

The Single Mother Diaries™, Volume Three:
Tips and Wisdom on Finding Love